Thomas Randolph

A summary View of the Laws relating to Subscriptions, etc.

With Remarks, humbly offered to the Consideration of the British

Parliament

Thomas Randolph

A summary View of the Laws relating to Subscriptions, etc.
With Remarks, humbly offered to the Consideration of the British Parliament

ISBN/EAN: 9783337153762

Printed in Europe, USA, Canada, Australia, Japan

Cover: Foto ©ninafisch / pixelio.de

More available books at **www.hansebooks.com**

A

SUMMARY VIEW

OF THE

LAWS

RELATING TO

SUBSCRIPTIONS, &c.

WITH

REMARKS,

HUMBLY OFFERED

TO THE CONSIDERATION OF THE

BRITISH PARLIAMENT.

LONDON:

PRINTED IN THE YEAR MDCCLXXI.

A

SUMMARY VIEW

OF THE

Laws relating to SUBSCRIPTIONS, &c.

WITH R E M A R K S,

Humbly offered to the Confideration of the
BRITISH PARLIAMENT.

[A] IN the Year 1553, were publifhed by the
King's Majefty's authority, "Articles
" agreed upon by the Bifhops and other learn-
" ed and godly men in the laft Convocation
" at *London*, in the year of our Lord 1552,
" to root out difcord of opinions, and efta-
" blifh the agreement of true religion."
Bifhop *Sparrow's* Collection of Articles, &c.

Remark.—It is however certain, that thefe
Articles were not agreed upon *in Convocation*.
Archbifhop *Cranmer's* account of the matter
was this. " I was ignorant of the fetting to of
" that title, and as foon as I had knowledge
" thereof, I did not like it; and when I com-
" plained thereof to the Council, it was an-
" fwered by them, That the Book was fo en-
" titled, becaufe it was fet forth in the time of
" the Convocation." *Burnet's* Hift. Reform.
Vol. III. p. 210, 211. And *Fox's* Martyrolo-
gy. —— Bifhop *Burnet* fays, " It feemed to be a
" great want, that this" [the publication of thefe

A 2   Articles]

Articles] " had been fo long delayed, as the
" old Doctrine had ftill the *legal* authority of
" its fide." What *legal* authority the old Doctrine had, except in the decifions of foreign
Canons which were received in this Kingdom
with great refervation of municipal Rights, &c.
is not clear. The danger of dogmatizing was
not unknown in thofe days, and it would have
anfwered the end of the new Eftablifhment juft
as well to have enjoined Subfcription to the
Article cited below in the Remark upon D
only.

[B] A Mandate bearing date *June* 19, in
the feventh year of the King's reign [1553]
was iffued, addreffed to the Officers of the
Archbifhop of *Canterbury* [*Cranmer*] (referring to a previous Mandate addreffed to the
Archbifhop himfelf, and giving him authority to expound, publifh, denounce, and
fignify the faid Articles to the King's clergy
and people within his jurifdiction) to fum-
mon or peremptorily admonifh all and fin-
gular Rectors, Vicars, Prefbyters, Stipendia-
ries, Curates, Rural Deans, Minifters, Mafters of Grammar Schools, public and pri-
vate Preachers of the Word of God, Lecturers and all who exercifed any Ecclefiaftical
function of whatever denomination, includ-
ing even Churchwardens, to appear at *Lam-
beth*, on *Friday* the 23d day of *June*, between the hours of feven and nine, to do
and

and receive what may be farther agreeable to reason, and becometh their duty to the royal dignity. *Burnet*'s Hift. Reform. vol. III. Collection, p. 202.

Rem. – This Mandate was iffued purfuant to a Letter of the Archbifhop's to the King and Council, " defiring that all Bifhops might have authority from the King to eaufe all Preachers, Archdeacons, Deans, Prebendaries, Parfons, Vicars, Curates, with all their Clergy, to fubfcribe the faid Articles."—The reafon given by the Archbifhop for fuch his defire was, " that " he trufted fuch a concorde and quietnefs in " Religion fhould fhortly follow thereof, as elfe " was not to be looked for of many Years." Probably the good man found this expedient did not anfwer his expectation. For tho' his Powers by this Mandate were very full, we find him declaring at his Examination before *Wefton*, that *he compelled no man to fubfcribe.* A Declaration that fufficiently fhews, he had met with oppofition to this meafure of *Peace* and *Quietnefs.* And moft probably it was not only the gentlenefs of his own difpofition, but the confcioufnefs of the incongruity of fuch compulfion, with the original principles of the Proteftant Reformation, which occafioned his Forbearance. This is one inftance of thofe difficulties the firft Reformers found in accommodating the new Eftablifhment to the temper of the times confiftently with their own Profeffions of being determined in matters of Faith and Doctrine, by the Scriptures only. It is hardly neceffary to
.obferve,

obferve, that fuch Expedients are not only ufe-
lefs now, but highly difparaging to the improve-
ments we pretend to in the prefent times.

[C] A particular Mandate to the Bifhop
of *Norwich*, bearing date *June* 9, directing
him to caufe the faid Articles to be fubfcribed by every manner of perfon prefented unto him to be admitted to any Ecclefiaftical Order, Miniftry, Office, or Cure
within his Diocefe, and if any man in that
cafe fhall refufe to confent to any of the
faid Articles, and to fubfcribe the fame,
then his Majefty willeth and commandeth
him the faid Bifhop, that neither he, nor
any for him, or by his procurement in any
wife, fhall admit fuch recufant or allow him
as fufficient or meet to take any Order, Miniftry, or Ecclefiaftical Cure. For which
his fo doing, his Majefty promifes to *dif-
charge* the Bifhop from all manner of pe-
nalties or dangers of actions, fuits, or pleas
of *Premunire, Quare impedit*, or fuch like.
Burnet, Ibid. p. 203.

Rem.—Here was a ftretch of the Royal Pre-
rogative which the end propofed would hardly
juftify. It was depriving the fubject of the benefit of the Law by an arbitrary *Non obftante.*
A writ of *Quare impedit* is a writ of *Right*,
and, without the Royal interpofition, would
have compelled the Bifhop to give the Clerk
inftitution,

institution, without some better Reason for denying it, than that the Clerk refused to subscribe these Articles.

[D] A Mandatorial letter from the Bishop of *Ely* (Goodricke) Chancellor, and three more appointed visitors of the University of *Cambridge*, dated *June* 1, 1553, addressed to Dr. *Sands* (probably Vicechancellor) and to the Regents and Non-Regents of the said University, enjoining an oath to be taken and subscribed by every Candidate for a degree in Divinity, or in Arts, containing, among others, the following engagement, *Deinde me Articulos de quibus in Sinodo Londinensi Anno Domini* 1553. *ad tollendam opinionum dissensionem, et consensum veræ Religionis firmandum inter Episcopos et alios eruditos viros convenerat et Regia Authoritate in lucem editos, pro veris et certis habiturum, et omni in loco tanquam consentientes cum verbo Dei defensurum, et contrarios Articulos in Scholis et Pulpitis vel respondendo vel concionando oppugnaturum.* Burnet, ubi supra, p. 205.

Rem.—In the former part of this oath the Candidate swore, *se veram Christi religionem omni animo complexurum, Scripturæ authoritatem Hominum judicio præpositurum, regulam vitæ et summam fidei ex verbo Dei petiturum. Cætera quæ ex verbo Dei non probantur, pro humanis et non necessariis habiturum.* It was utterly inconsistent

fiftent with the man's profeffing thefe things, to
affert, that he would efteem thefe Articles for
true and certain, and to defend them as fuch
againft all mankind, upon the mere prefump-
tion that they were agreeable to the word of
God.

[E] Upon Queen Elizabeth's acceffion,
an Act of Uniformity paffed, wherein is no
mention made of Subfcription either to the
Liturgy eftablifhed by that Act or to any
Articles of Religion, nor in the vifitatorial
Articles of Inquiry of the fame year, is
there any one intimating that fuch Subfcription was required. See *Sparrow's* Collection.

Rem.—It is remarkable that by this Statute,
the Clergyman offending againft it, is to be
lawfully convicted according to the Laws of
this Realm, by verdict of twelve men, or by
his own confeffion; or by the notorious evidence
of the fact; and was not left folely to the
Bifhop or Ordinary either for his trial or his punifhment; and as the words " and be thereof
" in form aforefaid lawfully convict," or words
equivalent, run through the whole Act, it was
manifeftly the intention of the Parliament to
put the inferior Clergy on the footing of the
reft of the free Subjects of the Realm, and not
leave them to the arbitrary cenfures of their re-
fpective Ordinaries, as thefe were too apt to en-
croach upon the civil powers, by exercifing
their

their jurisdiction, where the laws of the Realm should have restrained them, complaints of which were frequently made in Parliament, during this reign, and particularly with respect to Subscription, as will be seen by and by. N. B. There is one instance of a trial by Jury upon this Statute, before Lord Chief Justice *Catlin*, Bishop *Sandys*, &c. preserved in a Book, called *Part of a Register*, &c. p. 105. The Culprit was one *Robert Johnson*, Preacher at *Northampton*. He was indicted for administering the wine at the Communion without the words of Consecration, for marrying without the Ring, and baptizing without making the Sign of the Cross. He was convicted of the first offence, sentenced to suffer a year's imprisonment, and died in the Gate-house before the end of the year, *viz.* 1573. In the course of the Trial, and from the circumstances of *Johnson*'s Defence, some points of Doctrine were discussed, and *Johnson* was said to defend a horrible Heresy, which was probably the chief inducement with the Jury to find him Guilty. For the Fact, as *Johnson* shewed, was not against the Order of the Book. Subscription was hotly urged this year. But *Johnson*'s notion of the words of Institution, was not provided against in the Articles.

[F] In the year 1562. King Edward's Articles were revised, and altered, some things added, others taken away, and the number reduced to thirty-nine. At the end of which, is the following Ratifica-

tion.

tion. "This Book of Articles before re-
hearfed, is again approved, and allowed to
be holden and executed within the realm,
by the affent and confent of our Sovereign Lady *Elizabeth*, by the Grace of God
of *England*, *France* and *Ireland* Queen, De-
fender of the Faith, *&c*. Which Articles
were deliberately read, and confirmed again
by the Subfcription of the hands of the
Archbifhop and Bifhops of the upper
Houfe, and by the Subfcription of the
whole Clergy of the nether Houfe in their
Convocation in the year of our Lord 1571."

Rem.—The Latin Articles of 1562, differ
very much from thofe [Latin] Articles publifhed by Convocation in 1571. It is probable
there was the like difference between the Englifh
copies, nor is it poffible now to know which of
them is authentic. The Bifhops and Clergy in
1562, fubfcribed Archbifhop *Parker*'s Latin copy, and it is likely they fubfcribed a Latin copy revifed, in the Convocation of 1571. But the
Act of Parliament of that year refers to an Englifh book, and how that copy agreed with that
now in ufe, is totally unknown. It may be
faid however with great truth, that, on account
of the abovementioned differences, the articles
now fubfcribed, are not the Articles agreed
upon in the Convocation of 1562. There is
likewife a fallacy in the *Ratification* as it ftands
at prefent, with refpect to the Queen's confent,
as if both books of Articles were precifely the
fame,

fame, and equally *approved* by her Majefty; whereas the words fubjoined to the Latin Articles of 1562, fo far as the Queen's authority is concerned, are thefe, *Quibus omnibus Articulis fereniffima Princeps Elizabeth, Dei gratia Angliæ, Franciæ et Hiberniæ Regina, fidei Defenfor, &c. per feipfam diligenter prius lectis et examinatis, fuum affenfum præbuit*; which her Majefty might do without impofing Subfcription to them on her fubjects.

[G] In the year 1564 were publifhed, Advertifements partly for due order in the public adminiftration of the Sacraments, and partly for the Apparel of all perfons Ecclefiaftical. The Title of the laft fection is, " Proteftations to be made, pro-
" mifed and fubfcribed by them that fhall
" hereafter be admitted to any office, room
" or cure in any church, or other place
" Ecclefiaftical." Under this Title are the following Proteftations; " I fhall not preach or publicly interpret, but only read what is appointed by public authority, without fpecial licence of the Bifhop under his Seal. I do alfo faithfully promife in my perfon—to obferve, keep and maintain fuch order and uniformity in all external Policy, Rites and Ceremonies of the Church, as by the Laws, good Ufages and Orders, are already well provided and eftablifhed." *Sparrow's* Collection.

Rem.—

Rem.—What is here provided againſt, by this Proteſtation and Subſcription, was in a great meaſure ſecured by the Act of Uniformity, ſave in the Article of preaching and interpreting, concerning which there ſeems to have been no Law or Ordinance in being at that time, except the Queen's Injunctions of 1559; which were not underſtood then to have the force, or to make a part of the Laws of this Realm. Theſe advertiſements ſeem to have been calculated by Archbiſhop *Parker* to take the Clergy intirely into the hands of the Biſhops. What oppoſition theſe Advertiſements met with in the Queen's Council and elſewhere, and how diſtaſteful they were to many conſiderable men in different departments, may be ſeen in *Strype*'s Life of Archbiſhop *Parker*, Book 2. chap. xx.

[H] In the year 1571, An Act of Parliament paſſed injoyning Subſcription in theſe words; " Every perſon under the degree of a Biſhop which doth or ſhall pretend to be a Prieſt or Miniſter of God's Holy Word and Sacraments, by reaſon of any other form of inſtitution, conſecration or ordering, than the form ſet forth by Parliament in the time of the late King of moſt worthy memory, King *Edward* the ſixth, or now uſed in the reign of our moſt gracious Sovereign Lady, before the feaſt of the Nativity of *Chriſt* next following, ſhall in the preſence of the Biſhop

or

or the Guardian of the Spiritualities of
fome one Diocefe, where he hath or fhall
have Ecclefiaftical living, declare his affent, and fubfcribe to all the Articles of
Religion, which only concern the Confeffion of the true Chriftian Faith, and the
Doctrine of the Sacraments, comprifed in
a Book imprinted, intitled, *Articles where-
upon it was agreed*, &c. and fhall bring
from fuch Bifhop or Guardian of Spiritualities in writing, under his Seal authentic, a Teftimonial of fuch his Affent
and Subfcription, and openly on fome *Sun-
day* in the time of the public fervice afore-
noon in every Church, where, by reafon
of any Ecclefiaftical living he ought to
attend, read both the faid Teftimonial and
the faid Articles, upon pain that every fuch
perfon, which fhall not before the faid
feaft, do as is above appointed, fhall be
ipfo facto deprived, and all his Ecclefiaftical promotions fhall be void, as if he then
were naturally dead." *Statutes* 13 *Eliz.*
c. 12.

Rem.—The noble ftand made by the Houfe
of Commons in the reign of Queen *Elizabeth*
on divers occafions againft Ecclefiaftical encroachments, and in favour of Religious liber-
ty, plainly fhews, that the limiting the Subfcription of the Clergy to fuch Articles. " as
only concern the Confeffion of the true Chriftian

faith,

faith, and the doctrine of the Sacraments," in this Act, was no idle provifion, or words without meaning. Much has been faid concerning the uncertainty, what Articles were not to be fubfcribed under 'this reftriction, and an argument has been drawn from thence for an unlimited Subfcription. It appears however from the Converfation between Archbifhop *Parker* and Mr. *Peter Wentworth* in 1571, that the Articles for the Homilies, Confecrating of Bifhops and fuch like, were put out of the book, and were doubtlefs ftruck out in the copy annexed to the Bill. And as that copy is now irrecoverable, and as it hath been faid, feparated by fome unfair practice from the Act which refers to it, the Clergy muft be left to their own judgement, which of the Articles are or are not excepted in the Statute. Some learned and worthy perfons have thought that Subfcription to the 6th and 25th Articles is fufficient to fatisfy the intention of the Legiflature, the rather as the article which concerns the Homilies was certainly intended to be left out ; and therefore as moft of the doctrinal articles are but abridgements of what the Homilies treat of at more length, the Houfe of Commons had no more time to examine thofe Articles how they agreed with the word of God, than they had to examine the Homilies, as both muft have been examined together. It is only neceffary to obferve farther, that whatever Articles were enjoined by this Act to be fubfcribed, the fame and no other were to be read and affented to, as prefcribed by the
fubfequent

fubfequent Sections of this Statute. See *D'ewes*'s Journal, p. 239.

[I] In the fame year (1571.) the Bifhops put forth a Collection, intituled, *Liber quorundam Canonum Difciplinæ Ecclefiæ Anglicanæ, Anno* 1571. in which, under the Title *de Epifcopis*, it is ordained, that perfons approved for public preachers, fhould have their Licences renewed, *ita tamen ut prius fubfcribant articulis chriftianæ religionis publice in Synodo approbatis, fidemque dent fe velle tueri et defendere doctrinam eam quæ in illis continetur ut confentientiffimam veritati verbi divini.* And under the Title *Concionatores*, there is the following injunction. *Et quoniam articuli illi religionis chriftianæ in quos confenfum eft ab Epifcopis in legitima et fancta fynodo, juffu et authoritate fereniffimæ principis Elizabethæ convocata et celebrata haud dubie collecti funt ex facris literis veteris et novi Teftamenti, et cum cælefti doctrinâ quæ in illis continetur, per omnia congruunt; quoniam etiam liber publicarum precum, et liber de inauguratione archiepifcoporum, epifcoporum, prefbyterorum et diaconorum, nihil continent ab illa ipfa doctrina alienum, quicunque mittentur ad docendum populum, illorum articulorum, authoritatem et fidem, non tantum concionibus fuis, fed etiam fubfcriptione confirmabunt. Qui*

fecus

fecus fecerit, et contrariâ doctrina populum turbaverit, excommunicabitur. Sparrow's Collection.

Rem.—The intention of thefe Injunctions for Subfcription to the Articles, was to fupply, what the Bifhops thought the Parliament had left fhort, namely, to require a Subfcription to *all* the Articles, as appears by their making the Subfcriber affert their agreement with the word of God, and particularly mentioning the Book of Confecrating of Bifhops, &c. It is however certain, that the Queen never gave her Sanction to thefe Canons, and *Grindal* then Archbifhop of *York* " doubted whether they had *vigorem legis,*" [which out of all doubt they had not] " and " thought the Queen's *verbal* affent would not " ferve them, if they fhould be impleaded in " a Cafe of Premunire," in which he was very much in the right.

[K] In the year 1584. the Bifhops and Clergy of the Province of *Canterbury* affembled in Convocation, put forth a Collection intituled, *Articuli pro Clero,* in which it was injoyned, that no Bifhop fhould thereafter admit any perfon to Holy Orders, except he was of his own Diocefe, &c. *vel faltem, nifi rationem fidei fuæ juxta articulos illos Religionis in Synodo Epifcoporum et cleri approbatos latino fermone reddere poffit, adeo ut facrarum literarum teftimonia quibus*
eorundem

eorundem Articulorum veritas innititur recitare etiam valeat. Sparrow's Collection.

Rem.—Archbifhop *Whitgift* was now promoted to *Canterbury.* His predeceffor *Grindal* had complained greatly of the ignorance of the Clergy, and had ufed his utmoft endeavours to fupply the Church with abler men ; but generally without effect. By this time, it is likely, the Bifhops began to fee the impropriety of requiring Subfcription of poor Curates and Candidates for Orders to a fet of Articles of which they knew fo little ; and to obviate any reproach that might arife from this practice, enjoined the examination mentioned in thefe Canons. And had they ftuck to this expedient, it may eafily be imagined they muft not have ordained a Tithe of the Candidates who afpired to the Priefthood. Perhaps very few at this day would undertake to recite the teftimonies of Holy writ, on which the truth of thefe Articles depends. The Spirited Commons, however, became fenfible of this arbitrary impofition, and in the Parliament of 1585 petitioned the Houfe of Lords, among other matters relating to the Church, " That for the encourage-
" ment of many to enter into the Miniftry
" which are kept back by fome conditions of
" Oaths and Subfcriptions whereof they make
" fcruple, it may be confidered, whether this
" favour may be fhewed them, that hereafter
" no Oath or Subfcription be tendered to any
" that is to enter into the Miniftry, or to any
" Benefice with Cure, or to any place of preach-
" ing,

" ing, but fuch only as be exprefly prefcribed
" by the Statutes of this Realm ; fave only that
" it fhall be lawful for every Ordinary to try
" any Minifters prefented to any Benefice
" within his Diocefe by his Oath, whether he
" is to enter corruptly or incorruptly into the
" fame." *D'ewes's* Journal, p. 358. It is humbly prefumed, that the Anfwer of the Archbifhop of *York* to this reafonable Petition, is far
from being fatisfactory upon Proteftant principles.

[L] In the year 1597 were put forth,
Capitula five Conftitutiones Ecclefiafticæ, by
the Archbifhop, Bifhops, and Clergy of the
Province of *Canterbury* affembled in Con-
vocation, faid in the Title-page to be con-
firmed under the Great Seal of *England.*
In this collection, the requifite qualifica-
tion of Minifters, fo far as relates to the
Articles, is prefcribed in the fame words.
Sparrow's Collection.

Rem.—By this time Archbifhop *Whitgift* had
fo far eftablifhed his power that all oppofition
to his fyftem of Difcipline became fruitlefs even
in Parliament. *Strype* relates that, " a great
" heap of Grievances in the Church were thrown
" into the Parliament [of 1597] by Bills put in
" by divers perfons; but were not read, by
" means, no doubt, of fome higher influence."
Among others, " A grievance no way inferior
" to the former the ungodly ufe of the Statute
" of

" of 13 *Eliz.* concerning Faith and Sacraments,
" by which men are forced to Subfcription,
" and forced to accufe themfelves," i. e. by declaring their diffent from fuch Articles as did not
concern Faith and Sacraments. N. B. Thefe
Canons were confirmed under the Great Seal,
and they feem chiefly to aim at reforming fome
abufes in the Ecclefiaftical courts ; by way, one
may fuppofe, of precluding enquiries into fuch
matters, in Parliament. *Strype's* Life of *Whitgift*, p. 509.

[M] IN the year 1603, the Convocation
compofed the Book of Canons now in ufe,
the thirty-fixth of which injoyns Subfcription, 1. To the King's Supremacy. 2. To
the Book of Common Prayer, as containing
in it nothing contrary to the word of God.
3. To the thirty-nine Articles, acknow-
ledging all and every the faid Articles to be
agreeable to the word of God. Which
Subfcription is to be made in this form of
words. " I *N. N.* do willingly and *ex
animo* fubfcribe to thefe three Articles abovementioned, and to all that are contained in
them." The Royal affent to thefe Canons
is attefted under the Great Seal of *England* *.

Rem.—It is queftionable how far thefe Canons
are binding. Some great authorities fay, they have
no force with refpect to the Laity, and that they
bind the Clergy only by virtue of their Oath of

* See the G R A C E annexed.

Canonical

Canonical obedience, which however is limited
to *things lawful and honeſt*, and what is *lawful*
and *honeſt* in Canonical commands or injunctions
cannot *in equity* be determined before the Perſon
againſt whom the crime of diſobedience is committed. It is againſt the principles of juſtice,
and the genius of the Britiſh conſtitution, that
the ſame man ſhould be both judge and party.
Prohibitions from the temporal Courts lye
againſt the Courts eccleſiaſtical, in caſes which
concern the Clergy as well as the laity. Why
ſhould not the caſe of this Canonical Subſcription (as·the temporalities of beneficed·Clerks are
now made to depend upon a compliance with
it) be. ſubject to the verdict of twelve men, as
other caſes of leſs importance are made to be,
by the Act 1. *Eliz.* cap. 2 ? Very many of theſe
Canons are totally fallen into diſuſe, on account
of the impracticability of carrying them into
execution. Others, which might be executed,
are wholly neglected, poſſibly becauſe the execution of them might ſet the exerciſe of Canonical diſcipline in ſo many trifling matters, in
too odious a light. But can any thing be more
odious than to compel a learned and Proteſtant
clergy to ſubſcribe implicitly to all theſe anti-
quated propoſitions, on the pain of being ex-
cluded from the benefit of any temporal emo-
lument in the Church, where they might be of
the greateſt uſe to the people ?

[N] In the year 1613. A Grace was
paſſed by the Univerſity of *Cambridge*, in
conſequence of Letters from King *James* I.

prescribing Subscription to the three Articles
in the 36th Canon to the Candidates for the
Degree of Batchelor of Divinity, and of
Doctor in each faculty *.

[O] In the year 1616, the King *(James
I.)* sent directions to Dr. *John Hill*, then
Vice Chancellor, and the Heads of Houses
in the University of *Cambridge*, signifying
his pleasure that he would have *all* who
take any degree in the Schools, to subscribe to these Articles.

Rem.—Remarks on these Royal Directions,
will be found under the Letter [S].

[P] In the year 1628 King *Charles* I.
caused the 39 Articles to be republished,
prefixing thereto a *Declaration*, prohibiting
the least difference from the said Articles,
and consigning those who should affix any
new sense to any Article to the Church's
censure in his Majesty's Commission Eccle-
siastical, declaring that his Majesty would
see due execution done upon them.

Rem.—Nothing can be more inconsistent than
to continue this Declaration at the head of the 39
Articles, while every Subscriber is, by Canon 36,
confined to a particular invariable form of
words, in expressing his assent and consent to

* See the G R A C E annexed.

them;

them; nor can any judgment be made, where-
an article is ambiguoufly expreffed, which of the
fenfes given to it by different interpreters, may
be called *drawing it afide from the plain and full
meaning thereof:* Nor is the punifhment threatened,
for offences againft this declaration, now poffible
to be executed, as, thanks be to God and a virtu-
ous Legiflature, the Commiffion ecclefiaftical; to
which the Offender is configned for his cenfure,
is no longer in being.

[Q] IN the year 1640 were framed by
the Archbifhops, Bifhops, and Clergy in
Convocation, Conftitutions and Canons
Ecclefiaftical, in the fixth of which an Oath
is injoyned to be taken by all Archbifhops
and Bifhops and all other Priefts and Dea-
cons, all Mafters of Arts (the Sons of
Noblemen only excepted) all Batchelors
and Doctors in Divinity, Law or Phyfic,
all that are licenfed to practife Phyfic, all
Regifters, Actuaries and Proctors, all School-
mafters, all fuch as being Natives or natu-
ralized, do come to be incorporated into
the Univerfities here, having taken a degree
in any foreign Univerfity, " that they ap-
prove the Doctrine and Difcipline or Go-
vernment eftablifhed in the Church of *England,* as containing all things neceffary to
Salvation." *Sparrow's* Collection.

Rem.—For the objections made to this arbitrary

maxims of Civil and Ecclefiaftical policy which give a fanction to the Revolution of 1688, and to the Settlement of the Crown in the lineage of our moft gracious Sovereign, to whom and his Royal Houfe they profefs the moft fincere and cordial attachment. They fly for affiftance on the prefent occafion to that auguft Body, who have ever been the Protectors of the Rights and Privileges of the *Britifh* Subject, and who have in many periods of our Hiftory, from the firft dawn of Reformation, fhewn their care and concern to deliver the pious and confcientious Clergy, not only from the oppreffions of the Roman Pontiff, but from the attempts and encroachments of many in high places, whofe ambition difpofed them to eftablifh the like ufurpations, under a more plaufible pretext. The time is now come, they hope, when a candid hearing will be given to their reafonable and modeft Remonftrances, and all obftructions to their relief removed, which are founded in nothing, but a defire of exercifing a defpotic Rule over the Confciences, or in pretended fears and apprehenfions of Confequences, which can have no place, where the freedom folicited has no other object than the promotion of peace and unity, virtue and true piety among Clergy and People in the prefent ftate of things, and the everlafting Salvation of all in the world to come.

Upon the whole, the feveral Statutes enjoining Subfcription to the thirty-nine Articles are, in their prefent ftate, liable to different conftructions, particularly with refpect to the limitation in the Statute, 13 *Eliz.* c. 12.——And the Statute,

tute, 13 & 14 *Car.* II. commonly called the Act
of Uniformity, referring where Subfcription to
the Articles is by that Act enjoined, to the Statute of Queen *Elizabeth* before-mentioned ; it is
now become uncertain to which, or to how many
of the faid Articles, the Clergy are bound, by
the faid Statutes, to fubfcribe : And with refpect
to their Obligation to fubfcribe the faid Articles,
as a condition of holding their Temporalties, the
faid Uncertainty is not removed by the requifi-
tion of the 36th Canon to fubfcribe to *all* and
every the faid Articles, inafmuch as the faid Canon hath never been authorifed or confirmed by
Parliament ; and as by the Conftitution of this
Realm no Freehold can be paffed or legally held
by Virtue of the Canon Law only, as that would
give the Canon Law a paramount authority over
the common and ftatute Law of thefe Kingdoms,
and would be moreover an infringement of his
Majefty's Supremacy.

F I N I S.

APPENDIX:

Since the foregoing fummary View *was printed off, we have been favoured with the following account of the Origin of Subfcriptions to the* 39 *Articles and the* 36th *Canon, in the Univerfity of* Oxford.

" AFTER Queen *Elizabeth* had vifit-
" ed *Oxford*, feveral Regulations, re-
" fpecting Drefs and Difcipline, were by her
" recommended to the Univerfity. Ac-
" cordingly, in the year 1573, among
" many other Acts to put her Majefty's
" Reformation in execution, it was *decreed*
" *in Convocation*, That each Candidate for
" the future, previous to his taking his De-
" gree, fhould fubfcribe the Articles, as the
" form requires at prefent.

" Afterwards, in the year 1576, it was
" farther decreed, That every perfon above
" the age of fixteen, who entered his name
" in any College or Hall, fhould, before
" the *Friday* fe'nnight after his entrance, be
" matriculated, and then fubfcribe the Ar-
" ticles of the Church; and that the Vice-
D " chan-

" chancellor or Proctors fhould give him a
" certificate of having done fo.

" *Anthony Wood* fays, that the Puritans
" of thofe days complained fadly of this
" *unchriftian reftraint*; that many of them
" refufed to comply with it, and abfolutely
" fuffered themfelves to be deprived of their
" emoluments in the Univerfity.

" But whether it was owing to the oppo-
" fition of the Puritans, or becaufe thefe
" Decrees of Convocation were not armed
" with fufficient authority, this Subfcrip-
" tion foon came into difufe.

" In the year 1616 the Univerfity ap-
" plied to King *James*, for powers to make
" new Decrees to enforce Subfcription. The
" account which *Wood* gives of it, is as fol-
" lows:

" Having mentioned the founding of
" *Jefus* and *Wadham* Colleges, he adds, that
" this additional number of Colleges, con-
" tributed to the fpreading of Calvinifm;
" it was therefore intimated to the King,
" that there was danger that Prefbyterian-
" ifm would overrun the whole kingdom,
" if Students fhould imbibe the Principles
" of it along with the rudiments of acade-
" mical learning; and that this was the ra-
" ther to be apprehended, in that fo very
" few fubfcribed their affent to the three
" Articles contained in the 36th canon;
whence

" whence it would happen, that they who
" were difaffected to the ecclefiaftical go-
" vernment of the Church, and the Liturgy,
" and made no account of the other facred
" offices, would give their whole attention to
" Sermons; by which means thofe filly fel-
" lows, called *Lecturers*, would have an op-
" portunity of fpreading opinions directly
" contrary to the doctrine of the Church of
" *England.* Thefe things being infinuated
" to the King, he held a confultation with
" his Bifhops, and fome other Churchmen
" about him, on the 18th of *January*; and,
" after mature deliberation, tranfmitted cer-
" tain orders to the Vice-chancellor, fome
" Heads of Houfes, the Doctors of Divi-
" nity, and the two Proctors, requiring
" them to affift in the execution of them.
" The firft of them was, That every one ad-
" mitted to a Degree in the Univerfity
" fhould fubfcribe to the three Articles
" abovementioned. The execution of thefe
" orders was committed by the Earl of *Pem-*
" *broke*, newly made Chancellor of the
" Univerfity, to the Vice-chancellor, Heads
" of Houfes, and fome others, whom his
" lordfhip exhorted to put them in prac-
" tice with all diligence. And that thefe
" orders might not want the authority of
" Statutes, or rather might be reduced into
" the form of Statutes, certain Delegates

D 2   " out

" out of the Heads of Colleges were ap-
" pointed, who, by their joint labours and
" counsels, finished and issued, on the last
" day of *March*, the following Decrees.—
" With respect to the Articles of faith, it
" was decreed, that Subscription should be
" made in this form:

    " Ego A. (vel nos, A. B.) perlectis pri-
" us, vel ab alio coram me (vel nobis)
" recitatis Orthodoxæ fidei et Religionis
" Articulis xxxix, et in Sacra Synodo
" Londini habita A. D. 1562, constabi-
" litis, simulque tribus capitibus in alia
" Synodo Londinensi sub annum 1604 de-
" cretis, et in Canonem 36to. redactis,
" sciens volensque (seu scientes et volen-
" tes) ex animo subscribo (vel subscribi-
" mus.")

    " The present form of presenting people
" to their degrees was also at the same time
" appointed, to be said by their respective
" Deans, ending—Quem insuper scio legisse,
" vel lectos audivisse omnes articulos fidei
" quibus coram Procuratoribus subscripsit."

    " *Wood* says, that when these Statutes
" came to be published, they gave great of-
" fence to, and were considered as grievances
" by, the Puritans, and occasioned not a few
" invidious reflections upon Doctor *Laud*,
" as he was not only the adviser of these
" Articles" (meaning the particulars com-
3   prehended

prehended in thefe new Statutes) " but
" one of the delegates who framed the faid
" Statutes; to which however the Puritans
" conformed, though with reluctance, left,
" by flighting what was enjoined by the
" King's authority, they fhould expofe them-
" felves not only to expulfion, but to fome
" more grievous punifhment."

R E M A R K S.

All this, in the opinion of *Wood*, was ex-
tremely right, and as it fhould be. Paffing
by, however, the practifing in this manner upon
the King, and the views of diftreffing thofe who
were diftinguifhed by the name of *Puritans*
(views, worthy only of the wretched Policy of
thofe days) we may be allowed to examine what
legal authority thefe *injunctions* may be fuppofed
to have in the prefent times. It does not appear that Queen *Elizabeth* gave any particular
directions concerning Subfcription to the 39 Articles. This was merely the effect of a Decree
of the Univerfity affembled in Convocation.
The difufe of Subfcription, notwithftanding this
Decree, and the fubfequent application to King
James, difcover a confcioufnefs in the Governors
of *Oxford*, that a Decree of their Convocation
was void of authority to inforce Subfcription.
With refpect to King *James*'s Orders or Man-
dates, it does not appear, whether, by the word,
Edixit, we are to underftand a formal *Edict* in
writing, authenticated by the King's fign ma-
nual; or fome general directions, to put in execution what his Majefty would have decreed by
the

the Univerſity ; or laſtly, ſome verbal Orders given to their Chancellor, the Earl of *Pembroke*. It may be queſtioned, whether the Delegates, in reducing theſe Orders into the form of Statutes, did not exceed their Commiſſion ; or indeed, whether the Univerſity had any ſuch authority to delegate. For to whatever the Royal Mandate might amount, previouſly to the compoſing new Statutes, the academical doctrine *has been*, if I miſtake not, that no Statutes are binding upon them, which have not the Royal Aſſent or Ratification ; and nothing of that ſort appears from *Wood's* account, which, indeed, is very confuſed, and wants explanation in many particulars. If, on the other hand, our Univerſities have authority to *make* valid Statutes, without the Royal Ratification, they muſt have authority to *repeal* them. And yet this is what the *Cambridge* men lately denied, and thought moreover, that recourſe muſt be had to the *Legiſlature* to have ſuch Statute repealed or altered, tho' it has only the ſanction of a Grace paſſed in the Senate. Which ſuggeſts a queſtion, By what authority their predeceſſors aboliſhed the practice of requiring Subſcription from the Students at the time of their matriculation ? It ſhould be mentioned, to the honour of *Cambridge*, that there was no Subſcription required of the Students, or Candidates for Degrees, in that Univerſity, in the days of Queen *Elizabeth*; which I think amounts to a proof, that the Queen did not give any *particular* directions concerning that matter at either of the Univerſities, and that without ſuch directions, *Cambridge* did wiſely in not taking the Decree of *Oxford* for a precedent fit for them to follow. The authority, given by

King

King *James* to the Univerſity of *Cambridge*, in 1616, to require Subſcription of young Students, ſeems to be very weak. It is only *the ſignification of his Majeſty's pleaſure*, ſeconded by a letter from the Biſhop of *Wincheſter*, to the Vice-chancellor, which ſeems to leave much to the *option* of the Univerſity, the Heads of which did not, that I can find, ſollicit his Majeſty's directions on this behalf, after the example of *Oxford*. But, ſince the practice of requiring Subſcription of young Students, obtains at both Univerſities, it had been well if *Cambridge* had followed the example of *Oxford*, in taking care that the young Subſcribers ſhould either read the Articles, or hear them read, previous to their ſigning their aſſent to them. The formality with which this circumſtance is atteſted, by the perſon who preſents the Candidates at *Oxford*, ſhould ſeem to imply more than a bare reading ; ſomething, perhaps, like an explanatory Lecture upon theſe Articles. But this is conjecture ; and, by an eaſy figure, *reading* may include *underſtanding* them. Indeed, as reading the Articles before taking the firſt Degree, would be a novelty at *Cambridge*, ſome of the young ſophiſters might be pert enough to aſk queſtions, or form ſyllogiſms upon particular paſſages, which it might take more time to anſwer than could well be ſpared at the buſy ſeaſon of conferring Degrees. And probably they who have the ordering of ſuch things, may think it ſufficient to ſay, *They may read the Articles if they will. No-body hinders them. If they do not, it is their own fault.* This is eaſily ſaid ; but ſome people may be of opinion, that, be the *legal* obligation to ſubſcribe what it may, there is a point

of

of *equity* inseparable from such cases as this, namely, That they who undertake the education of these young men, should not content themselves with knowing that they have *read* these Articles. If they will have Degrees, it is not at their option whether they will subscribe them or not. Must not honest and conscientious Tutors and Governors be sensible, that it pertaineth to the faithful discharge of their offices, to instruct these young men in the Doctrines of these Articles, to apprize them of the nature and tendency of Subscription, and to give satisfactory answers to such doubts or difficulties as the sense and apprehension of the Candidates may suggest to them? The whole affair is too melancholy to be farther dwelt upon. Let us blush for what is past, and unite our endeavours, that these shameful blemishes in our discipline, may be no longer our *opproòrium*.

F I N I S.

www.ingramcontent.com/pod-product-compliance
Lightning Source LLC
Chambersburg PA
CBHW032143080426
42733CB00008B/1179